ARITHMETRIX

by

Charlie and Becky Daniel

Copyright © Good Apple, Inc., A Division of
Frank Schaffer Publications, Inc. 1980

ISBN No. 0-916456-75-7

GOOD APPLE, INC.
23740 Hawthorne Boulevard
Torrance, CA 90505-5927
A Division of
Frank Schaffer Publications, Inc.

All Rights Reserved – Printed in the United States of America
by Production Press, Inc., Jacksonville, Illinois.

TABLE OF CONTENTS

FLOW CHARTS

DIRECTIONS: Read the input number. Follow the chart and arrive at the output number.

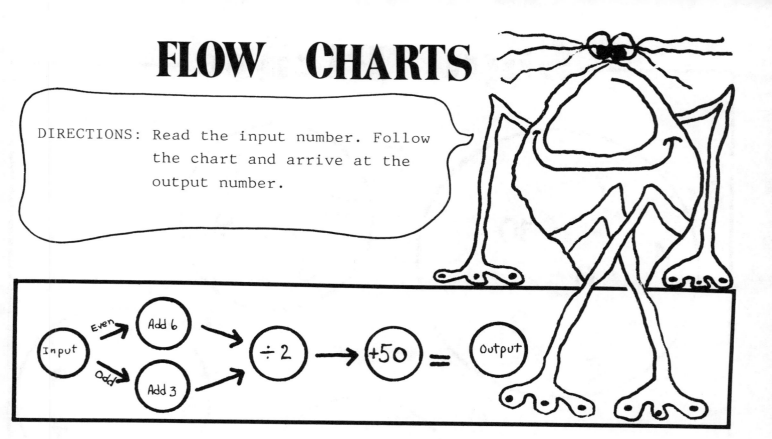

Input	Output	Input	Output
5		19	
7		8	
10		57	
2		100	
3		35	
11		70	
50		0	
33		44	

DIRECTIONS: Make up your own flow chart. Give a friend an input number and see if he can arrive at the correct output number.

Sign Please

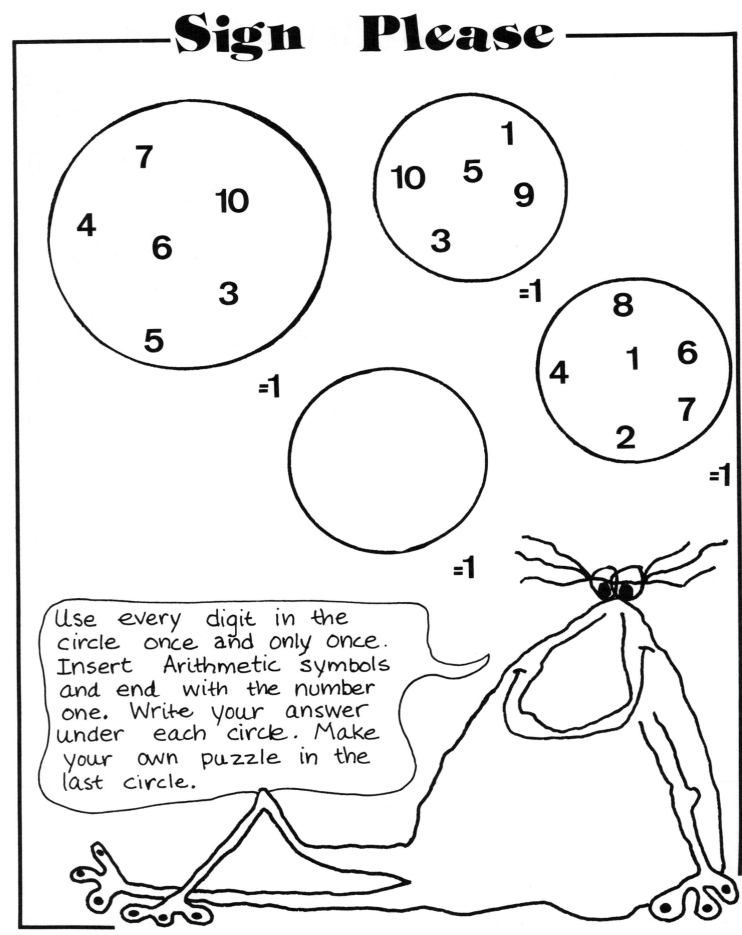

7
10
4
6
3
5

=1

1
10 5
9
3

=1

8
1 6
4
7
2

=1

=1

Use every digit in the circle once and only once. Insert Arithmetic symbols and end with the number one. Write your answer under each circle. Make your own puzzle in the last circle.

chart it

Study the first example, then complete the chart. Put in checks and write each equation.

	1	4	16	64
20 = 4 + 16		✓	✓	
70 =	✓✓	✓		✓
33				
40				
99				
130				
88				
18				
36				
207				
400				
876				
67				
193				

3

ADDS UP

	1	4	16	64
	✓	✓	✓	
	✓✓			✓
		✓✓✓	✓	✓
	✓	✓✓✓		
		✓✓✓	✓✓✓	✓✓
	✓✓✓	✓✓	✓✓	✓✓
	✓	✓✓✓		✓✓✓
	✓✓✓	✓✓✓		
	✓	✓✓	✓✓✓	✓✓✓
			✓✓	✓✓✓
	✓✓✓	✓	✓✓✓	✓✓✓

This page is like the last one, except the checks are shown. You must find the answer. Write each equation, too!

BIG 19

DIRECTIONS: All you need to do is write 9 equations that all result in the answer 19. This is the catch: the first line must contain only the numeral one. The second line must contain only the number two, the third line three, etc. You may never use more than seven numbers in any one line. Insert the correct arithmetic signs into each equation. The first one is done for you.

1. 11 + 11 - 1 - 1 - 1 :19

2. :19

3. :19

4. :19

5. :19

6. :19

7. :19

8. :19

9. :19

alphabet arithmetic

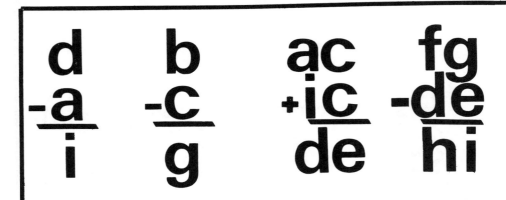

$$
\begin{array}{r} d \\ -a \\ \hline i \end{array}
\qquad
\begin{array}{r} b \\ -c \\ \hline g \end{array}
\qquad
\begin{array}{r} ac \\ +ic \\ \hline de \end{array}
\qquad
\begin{array}{r} fg \\ -de \\ \hline hi \end{array}
$$

Each letter in the equations above stands for a different digit: 1, 2, 3, 4, 5, 6, 7, 8, or 9. They are the same in all 4 problems above. <u>HINT</u>: C=4

Can you figure out what number each letter stands for?	Make up your own alphabet arithmetic code. Give a friend two or three true equations using your code. See if your friend can break your code.

a __

b __   **f** __

c __   **g** __

d __   **h** __

e __   **i** __

GUZ-AFTA

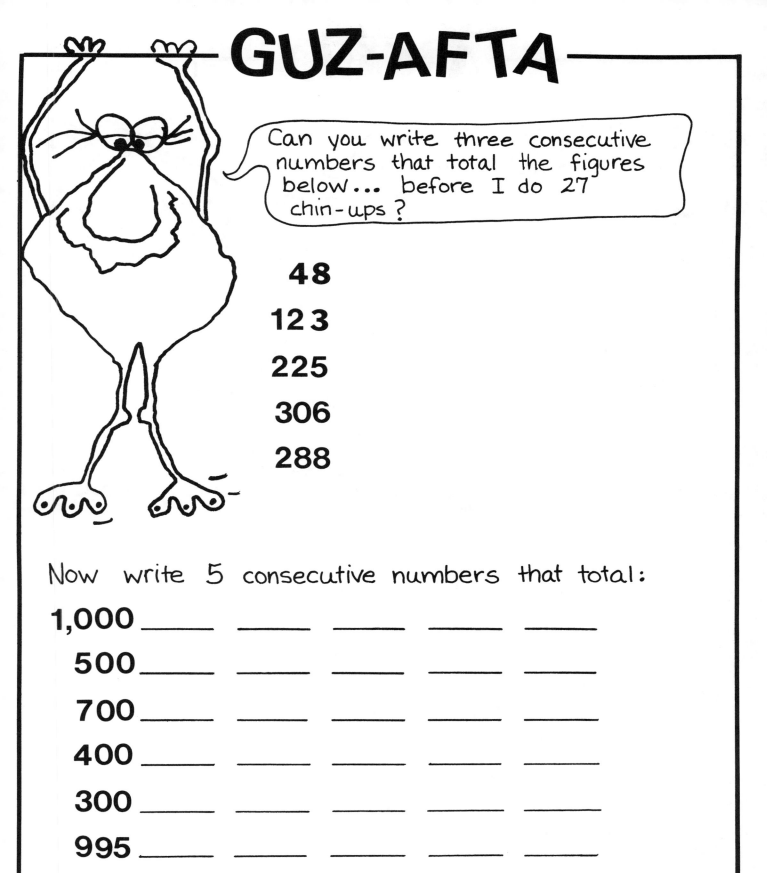

Can you write three consecutive numbers that total the figures below... before I do 27 chin-ups?

48

123

225

306

288

Now write 5 consecutive numbers that total:

1,000 _____ _____ _____ _____ _____

500 _____ _____ _____ _____ _____

700 _____ _____ _____ _____ _____

400 _____ _____ _____ _____ _____

300 _____ _____ _____ _____ _____

995 _____ _____ _____ _____ _____

15 _____ _____ _____ _____ _____

A CELL

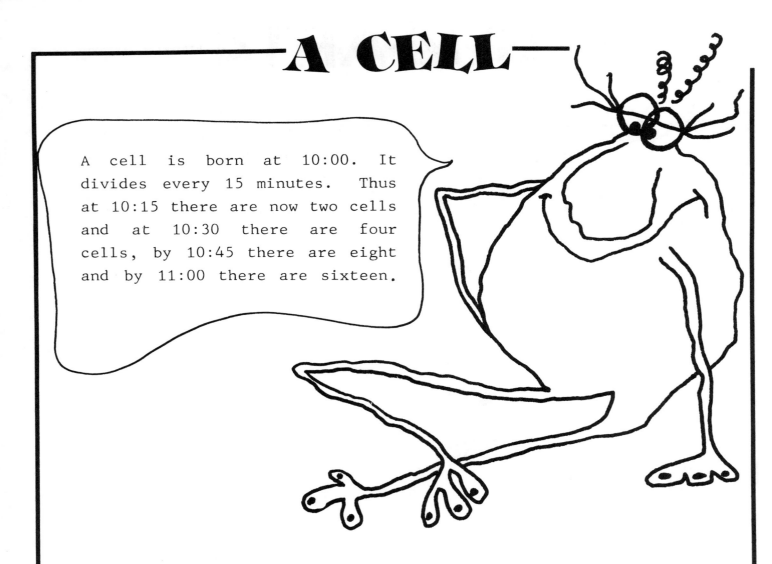

A cell is born at 10:00. It divides every 15 minutes. Thus at 10:15 there are now two cells and at 10:30 there are four cells, by 10:45 there are eight and by 11:00 there are sixteen.

1. How many cells are there at 11:00?_____

2. How many cells are there at 12:15?_____

3. At what time are there 8,192 cells?_____

4. How many cells are there by 3:00? _____

5. At what time will there be over one million cells? _____

6. How many cells will there be at 3:15?_____

7. How many cells will there be at 4:00?_____

8. How many cells will there be at 4:30?_____

9. At what time will there be over a half-million cells?_____

10. How many cells will there be by 5:00?_____

PUZZLERS

1. Can you arrange 8 eights so that they will total 1000? _____

2. Can you write an equation using 4 fours that will total 9? _____

3. What three digits have the same sum and the same product? _____

4. Using the same number three times, can you write the number 15? _____

5. Write down an odd number using only even digits.

   _____

6. Putting in only arithmetic signs, can you make these numbers total 100?

   1   2   3 4 5 6 7   = 100

These are more difficult. Take your time.

9

Stumpers

DIRECTIONS: In each row the problems are followed by a string of numbers. Hidden within those numerals is the answer or an equation that is equal to the answer. Circle the answer or equation for each problem. If it is an equation, insert the needed arithmetic sign(s).

EXAMPLE:

4 x 4 =   9   7   2   4   (1   6)   7   8   9

5 x 5 =   9   3   (2   0 + 5)   6   3   4

- -

6 x 19 =   8   0   4   1   4   1   1   4   3   3   7

7 x 75 =   7   5   0   0   2   0   5   7   8   9   6

1000 − 1 =   7   8   9   1   1   6   1   1   1   9   7

15 x 15 =   0   0   4   5   5   6   7   2   0   9   8

492 ÷ 6 =   9   8   0   4   1   2   5   6   7   7   8

441 + 141 =   5   8   3   9   0   1   9   2   6   7   8

1143 + 1945 =   1   6   1   9   3   7   3   0   0   6   8

88 x 37 =   8   1   6   2   6   4   0   5   9   6   7

1000 + 50 =   7   8   7   5   1   4   6   8   9   1   3

196 ÷ 14 =   7   2   4   6   8   7   1   7   4   5   9

10

THE MATCH

Name	Total						
Ted	206	45	45	39	39	19	19
Jeff	192	45					
Mitch	180			39			
Ann	242			45			
Eddie	252	45					

At the annual archery match, these five children were the finalists. Their total scores are listed in the second column. Each finalist got six shots. Looking at the total scores, can you figure the six shots each person made?

The first one is done for you!

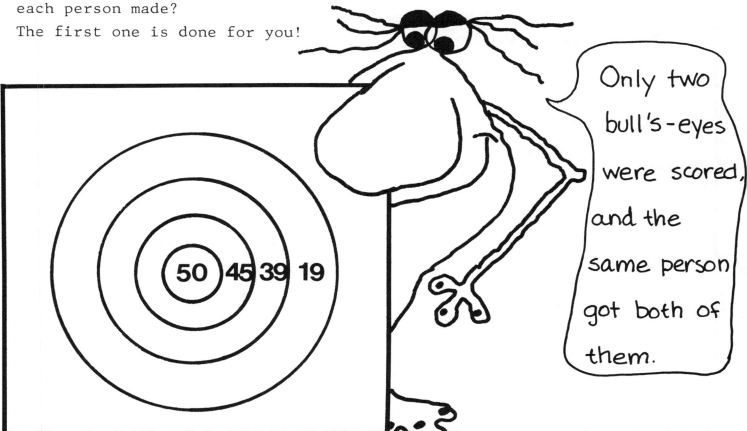

Only two bull's-eyes were scored, and the same person got both of them.

ONLY FOUR

Find a four digit number that can be divided by the numbers 2, 3, 4, 5, 6, 7, 8, and 9, and will always have a remainder of 1 in the answer.

ONE HINT: Two of the digits are the numeral 2, and the other two numbers are odd.

Use this space to try number combinations.

Mystery Numbers

Look at the equations below. Can you figure out what letter is used to represent the numerals 0-9?

$$x + x = x$$
$$h + h = n$$
$$h + x = h$$
$$g + w = z$$
$$z - q = h$$

$$h + v = hx$$
$$h + f = v$$
$$w + h = j$$
$$j + j = hx$$
$$n + g = j$$

Write the letters that stand for each numeral.	After you solve the code, write some equations in code.
0 5	
1 6	
2 7	
3 8	
4 9	

THE COST OF IT

DIRECTIONS: Three hats and one pair of shoes sold for the same as two dresses. One hat, two pairs of shoes and three dresses sold together for $25.00. What was the price of the hats, the shoes and the dresses?

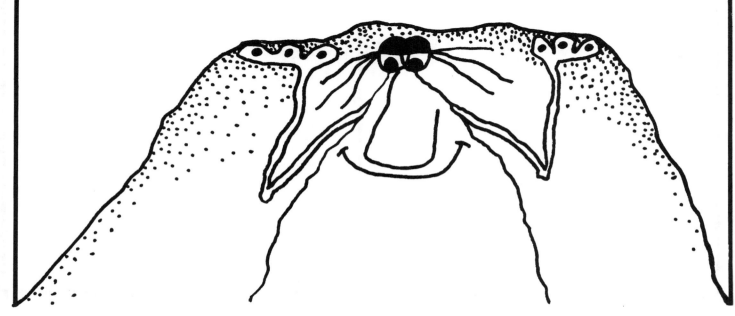

short trip

Mork plans to drive to a city some 200 kilometers away from his home. After travelling 50 kilometers, he picks up a friend. His friend rides to the city with him. The next day he drops his friend off at the same place where he picked him up. He then drives the rest of the way home. Mork's friend agrees to share the gasoline expenses which were $35.00 for the entire trip.

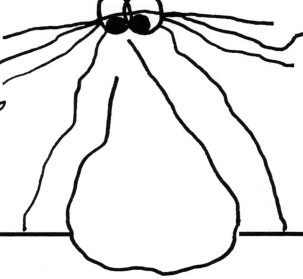

It might help to draw a picture of the trip. Mark it off in Kilometers.

1. How much do you think Mork's friend should pay? $_____

2. How much should Mork pay? $_____

3. How many kilometers does his friend ride in all?_____

4. How many kilometers does Mork drive by himself during the trip?_____

5. How much does each man pay to travel one kilometer?_____

6. What fractional part of the trip does Mork travel by himself? _____

A TRADE

I went to market to sell 50 animals. I sold horses for $20 each. I sold cows for $10 each. Chickens I sold for only $5 each.

I came home with exactly $500 in my pockets.

How many horses did I sell? _____

How many cows did I sell? _____

How many chickens did I sell? _____

EXACT CHANGE

DIRECTIONS: The object of this game is to make an exact amount of money with a given number of coins, bills or a combination of both coins and bills. Each player rolls the dice twice. The first roll determines the amount of money to be made. The second roll tells the number of coins, bills or a combination of both that must be used.

EXAMPLE: A player rolls a 6 and a 5 on his first roll.
He then rolls a 1 and a 2 the second roll.
Thus, the player must give a combination of 3 coins, 3 bills or a combination of both that equals $11.00.

ANSWER: One ten-dollar bill and two 50¢ pieces.

Before you play the game, work the examples below.

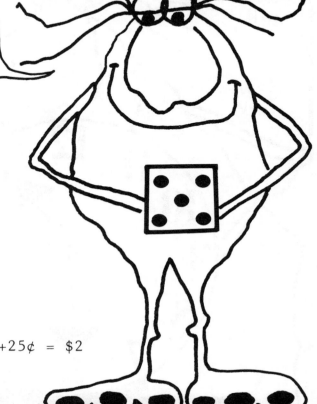

first roll: 3,6
second roll: 3,2
answer: $5+$1+$1+$1+$1 = $9

first roll: 2,4
second roll: 1,4
answer: $5+25¢+25¢+25¢+25¢ = $6

first roll: 6,5
second roll: 1,2
answer: $5+$5+$1 = $11

first roll: 1,1
second roll: 3,5
answer: 25¢+25¢+25¢+25¢+25¢+25¢+25¢+25¢ = $2

17

strikes again

1. There is a clock that strikes once on each half hour. It also strikes once at one o'clock, twice at two o'clock, three times at three o'clock, etc. It takes one second for each strike. How many minutes is the clock actually striking during a twenty-four hour period?

2. How many times in 24 hours does the clock strike once three times in a row?_____ At what times of the day does the clock strike one time on three different occasions in a row during a 24-hour period?_____

_____

Make up your own clock problem below. See if a friend can solve your puzzle.

CAMP KAZOOWA

DIRECTIONS: Read the story below. You may need to make a picture in order to keep the times properly in mind. Then answer the questions that follow.

Mary leaves the campground at 9:00 and walks to the lake which is exactly two miles away. She returns at 11:00.

Jim leaves the campground at 10:00 and runs to the lake. He also returns at 11:00.

----

1. How many miles per hour did Mary walk?_____

2. How many miles per hour did Jim run?_____

3. How many times will Jim pass Mary during his trip?_____

4. At approximately what time will the two children pass one another?_____

5. At 10:15 will Mary be walking to or from the lake?_____

6. At 10:15 will Jim be running to or from the lake?_____

7. Who will get to the lake first?_____

8. Which of the children will arrive at the lake at approximately 10:30?_____

9. At 10:30 who will have 3/4 of the trip completed?_____

10. At 10:45 who will have 3/4 of the trip completed?_____

EGGS

It takes ten hens one week to lay fifty eggs.

1. How many eggs will sixty hens lay in four weeks?

2. How many eggs will five hens lay in two weeks?

3. How long will it take sixty hens to lay 100 dozen eggs?

4. How long will it take twenty-five hens to lay 500 eggs?

5. How long will it take six hens to lay 300 eggs?

Ages ???

Bob's sister Becky is twelve years old. His father is six times Bob's age. In ten years Bob will be four years older than his sister is today.

1. In 30 years how old will Bob be? _____

2. How old is Bob today? _____

3. What will be the total age of Bob, his sister Becky and his father in ten years? _____

4. In how many years will Bob's sister Becky be as old as her father is today? _____

5. In how many years will Bob's father be 56 years old? _____

6. In how many years will Bob's sister be 42? _____

7. How old was Bob's father when Bob was born? _____

8. How old was Bob's sister Becky when Bob was born? _____

9. When Bob is 17, how old will his father be? _____

10. When Bob is 25, how old will his sister be? _____

This one is too hard for me.

HOW OLD ?

DIRECTIONS: A man named Andrew has a wife named Ruth. They have three children named Kathy, Tim and Rose.

The difference between Andrew's age and his wife's age is the same as the difference between Kathy's and Tim's ages.

Andrew is five times the age of his daughter Rose.

Ruth is five times the age of her son Tim.

The total age of all five people is 65 years.

How old is Andrew?_____   How old is Tim?_____

How old is Ruth?_____   How old is Rose?_____

How old is Kathy?_____

Use this box below to figure your answers.

FRACTIONS

Look at the total rectangle. Figure out what each fractional part is represented by each letter. Example: a = 1/8.

a =　　d =　　g =

b =　　e =　　h =

c =　　f =　　i =

23

SUPER SNAPS

DIRECTIONS: A certain cereal called Super Snaps is sold in both sugar-coated and plain varieties. Six hundred people were asked questions about Super Snaps. One third of them admitted that they had never tasted Super Snaps. One sixth of the people interviewed said that they had bought them only in the sugar-coated form. One twelfth had always bought plain Super Snaps. The rest of the people bought them plain sometimes and sugar-coated on other occasions.

1. How many people interviewed had never tasted Super Snaps?_____

2. How many bought Super Snaps sugar-coated?_____

3. How many people always bought Super Snaps plain?_____

4. How many people bought them both plain and sugar-coated?_____

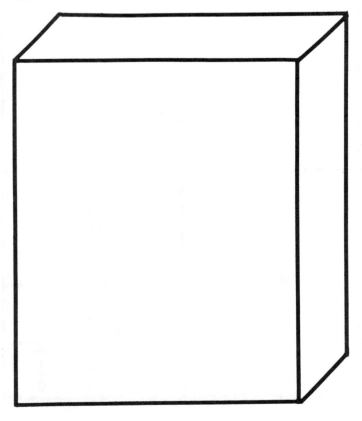

Design the Super Snap box.

OH BEANS

Four children are holding a total of 56 beans. Using only the clues provided below, determine how many beans each child is holding.

1. Betty has six times as many as Mary.

2. George has twice as many as Peter.

3. Peter has seven times as many as Mary.

Peter has_____

Mary has _____

George has _____

Betty has _____

Here are four clues that are needed to solve this math puzzle. Read them very carefully and then determine how many of each farm animal the farmer has.

1. There are just half as many cats as there are dogs.

2. There are exactly half as many chickens as horses.

3. There are three times as many chickens as dogs.

4. There are 21 animals altogether.

dogs_____   horses_____

cats_____   chickens_____

MILK

DIRECTIONS: John had a carton that was 1/3 full of chocolate milk. Marvin had a carton that was one-half full of chocolate milk. Fred's carton contained only one-fourth of the contents of a full carton of milk. Each boy filled his carton full of white milk. The boys then poured all three cartons of milk into a tall pitcher. They then poured each of them a glass of milk. What fractional part of the milk was chocolate? _____ What fractional part was white?_____

What equation is needed to find the answer? Write it below.

SISTERS

DIRECTIONS: Three sisters bought a 24-ounce bottle of cologne. They wanted to share the cologne evenly. When they got home, they discovered that the only bottles they had were a 5-ounce bottle, an 11-ounce bottle and a 13-ounce bottle. How could they divide the cologne evenly? Perhaps the chart below will help you

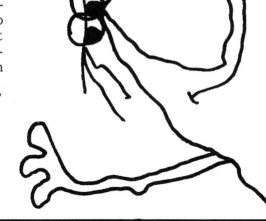

	24 oz.	13 oz.	11 oz.	5 oz.
	24	0	0	0

It is possible to solve this puzzle in six steps.

A RECORD

DIRECTIONS: Compute the number of grooves on a particular record.

Donna has a new Beatles record. It has a circumference of 18 inches. Each time the record makes a complete revolution, the circumference of the groove is 1/8 inch shorter. There are nine songs on the record. It takes 160 revolutions for each song to play. How many grooves are there on the record?

Use the space below to compute your answer.

7,985,340

8 SONS

A man named Frank owned sixteen houses located on eight acres of land. In his will he left an equal number of houses, and amount of land to each of his eight sons. Draw lines to show how the land and houses may be equally divided.

X   X   X

X   X

X

X

X   X   X

X   X
X

X

X

X   X

DONUTS

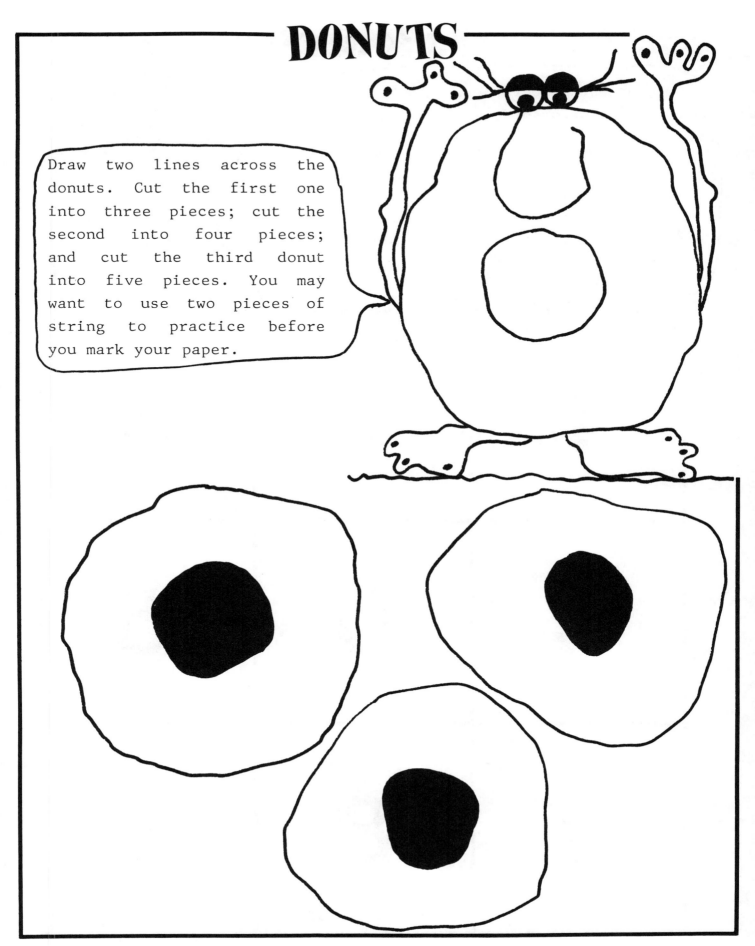

Draw two lines across the donuts. Cut the first one into three pieces; cut the second into four pieces; and cut the third donut into five pieces. You may want to use two pieces of string to practice before you mark your paper.

31

JUGGLE

Cut out the numbers below and shift them around to solve the puzzles.

1. Make two straight lines of numbers, each with five cards that have the same total.

2. Divide the cards into three groups, each having the same number of cards and the same total.

1	2	3
4	5	6
7	8	9

TOTAL 18

Arrange the numerals 1-9 in the circles so that each of the four lines of three circles has a total of 18.

60 Is It

Write the numerals 1-9 in the circles so that a total of four lines of three circles has a total of 60.

TWENTY

Fill in the circles with the digits 1-9 so that the sum of the digits on each side of the triangle is 20.

Draw your own triangle and circle design like the one below on the back of this sheet. Fill in the circles with the digits 1-9 so that the sum of all three sides equals 17.

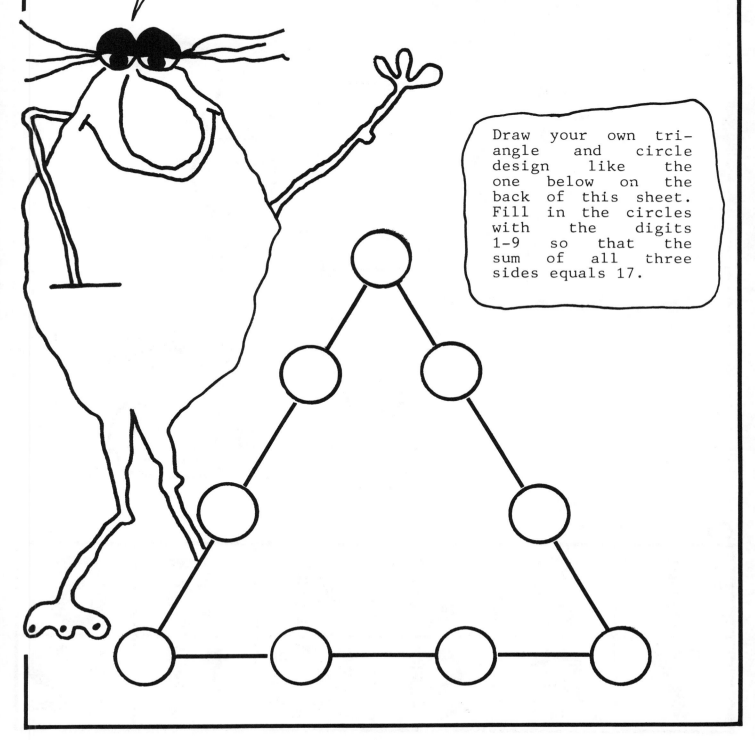

26?

Find a way to place the numerals 1-12 in the circles so that the four circles in each of the six rows add up to a total of 26.

Cut out these numerals:

1	2	3	4	5	6
7	8	9	10	11	12

30 IS PERFECT

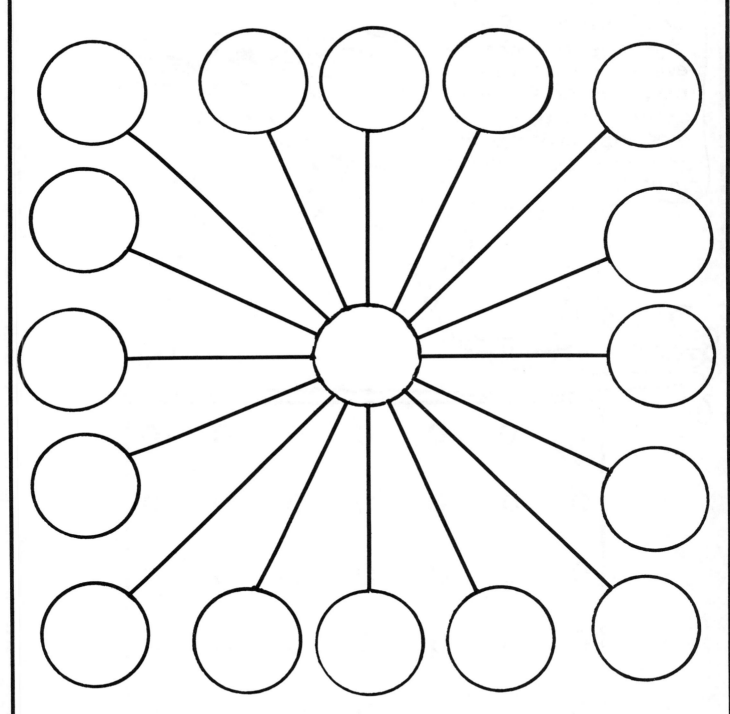

Place the digits 2-18 in the circles so that each of the three circles that is connected by a line adds up to a total of 30. Use the back side of this paper to practice different combinations before marking your paper.

JUST 11

Start at any circle. Draw twelve straight lines, across, down, or diagonally. The object is to connect every circle. Lines may not cross each other. You may not pick up your pencil once you start making your lines.

CONNECT

Draw lines to connect the 5 to the 5, the 6 to the 6, the 7 to the 7, the 8 to the 8, and the 9 to the 9. You may not cross any lines. You may want to use some pieces of string to practice. When you have discovered the answer, draw in the five correct paths.

0	8	0	0	0	0	0	0
0	0	7	0	0	5	0	0
0	0	0	0	0	0	0	0
0	0	0	0	0	0	0	0
0	0	0	0	6	0	0	7
0	0	9	0	0	0	0	9
0	0	0	0	0	5	0	0
6	0	0	8	0	0	0	0

DOTS

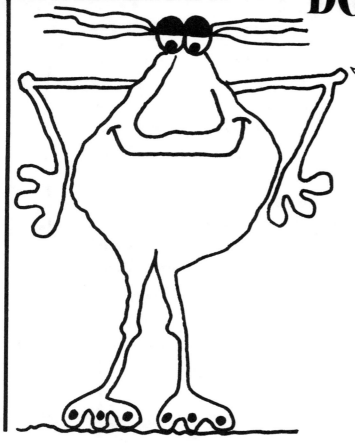

Draw or make eleven dots that form five straight lines with four dots in each line. You will need lots of scratch paper to practice. Write the solution in the box below.

This example below is wrong because if you connect the dots across and down, you will have made 8 lines with four dots in each, but you used too many lines.

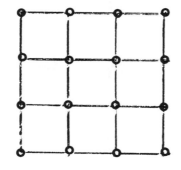

CAN YOU?

Can you draw five straight lines so that every X is in a separate enclosure?

crescent

Draw five straight lines and divide the crescent moon into as many pieces as you can. Try to make more pieces than there are in the example shown, which has been made into 14 sections. Can you possibly make yours into 20 sections?

Experiment by drawing other crescent shapes on the back before you work on the examples below.

EXAMPLE:

TOTAL: _____

TOTAL: _____

Nine children form a circle to choose a leader. They count off to seven with the seventh person being required to step out. The children repeat this process until only one person is left. That person is the leader. Name the children: A, B, C, D, E, F, G, H, I. If they start with A and work around the circle alphabetically, which student will be the leader?_____

Where should they start if G is to win?_____

Where should they start if I is to win?_____

If they start with A, which child will go out first? _____, second_____, third_____, fourth _____, fifth_____, sixth_____?

Use these circles in helping to work out the answers. Make up a question of your own. Write it down and see if a friend can figure out the answer to your question.

PROBABILITY

DIRECTIONS: Roll a pair of dice 100 times. Each time you roll, mark a tally line in the appropriate square. For example, the roll of 6 and 2 is already tallied for you.

	1	2	3	4	5	6
1						
2						
3						
4						
5						
6		I				

Which number combination came up most often?_____

What was the average number for most number combinations?

44

BINGO

DIRECTIONS: To play this game, each person will need a score sheet and 35 beans or paper markers. Before the game begins each player inserts in the boxes of the score sheet at random any numbers from 1-36. The player may not have any number repeated on his or her card. There will not be room for every number from one to thirty-six.

The first player then rolls the dice. He or she may add the two numbers, subtract the smaller from the larger, or multiply the two numbers. The player then calls out the sum, the difference or the product. All players look to their card to see if they have that number. If they do, they may cover it with a bean or marker. The game continues until one player has covered five numbers in a line, either across, down or diagonally.

To extend the game, play until all players have covered the five numbers in a row or you can play until each player has covered all of the numbers on his or her card.

BINGO

		FREE		

TWENTY WINS

DIRECTIONS: The first player rolls the dice. He can either add or subtract the two numbers that are shown on the dice. Next, the player enters the sum or difference anywhere on the score sheet. The second player then does the same thing. The game continues until one of the players can successfully put four digits together into a square that totals 20. That player then gets a point.

The game continues until one player has received a given number of points or until the board is full of numbers.

Example:

5	6	7	6	
5	4	3	4	

FINGER RACES

The word digit comes from the Latin word meaning "fingers."
Our ten fingers were truly the first "digital computers."

DIRECTIONS: Two players stand facing each other with their
hands behind their backs. They count together: "one, two
and three." On the count of "three," they both extend one
to ten fingers in front of them.

Both players then race to calculate the three-part problems.

Step #1:   They add the two numbers.

Step #2:   They then subtract the smaller number from the
                  larger number.

Step #3:   They then multiply the answer from step one by
                  the answer from step two.

The first person to shout out the correct answer is the
winner. If a player shouts out an incorrect answer, the
other player gets the point and the players start a new
round. If the players desire, someone can keep track of
points to see who gets the most points in a given time
or who gets a given number of points first.

Example: If the two players show the numbers 7 and 3

Step #1:   7 + 3 = 10

Step #2:   7 - 3 = 4

Step #3:   10 x 4 = 40

The first player to shout "40" is declared the winner.

Before you play the game, work the two examples below:

6   5   8   4

Step #1:   Step #1:

Step #2:   Step #2:

Step #3:   Step #3:

WHISTLE

DIRECTIONS: The first player announces a number from 2-9. Then, for the remainder of the game, all participants must avoid mentioning that number as they count off. As the players take turns counting off from 1-100, they must whistle when they come to a multiple of that number.

For example: If the number chosen is 5, the game might well sound like this: 1, 2, 3, 4, whistle, 6, 7, 8, 9, whistle, whistle, 11, 12, 13, 14, whistle, whistle, whistle. The players must whistle the number of times the 5 is found in that number.

When a player makes a mistake by calling out the number that should be whistled, or he whistles a number that is not a multiple of the chosen number, he drops out of the game. The game continues until only one member remains in the circle. That person is then declared the winner.

When players get very good at this game, it can be played by having students count by 2's, 5's or 10's. Or, they may want to count by the odd numbers.

Let the children think up new rules of their own on variations of the whistle-multiplication game.

21 ROLLS

Object: To get as many points as possible

Materials: One pair of dice plus a score card for each player

Directions: Players take turns rolling the dice. As the players roll the various number combinations, they mark them on the score sheet and receive the appropriate points. If a player rolls a number combination which he already has, that player must then take a score of zero in the space of his choice. After 21 rolls, the players total their points to determine who has the highest score.

1,1 = 2 points		3,3 = 6 points	
1,2 = 3 points		3,4 = 7 points	
1,3 = 4 points		3,5 = 8 points	
1,4 = 5 points		3,6 = 9 points	
1,5 = 6 points		4,4 = 8 points	
1,6 = 7 points		4,5 = 9 points	
2,2 = 4 points		4,6 = 10 points	
2,3 = 5 points		5,5 = 10 points	
2,4 = 6 points		5,6 = 11 points	
2,5 = 7 points		6,6 = 12 points	
2,6 = 8 points		Total	
Total		GRAND TOTAL	

CROSS OUT

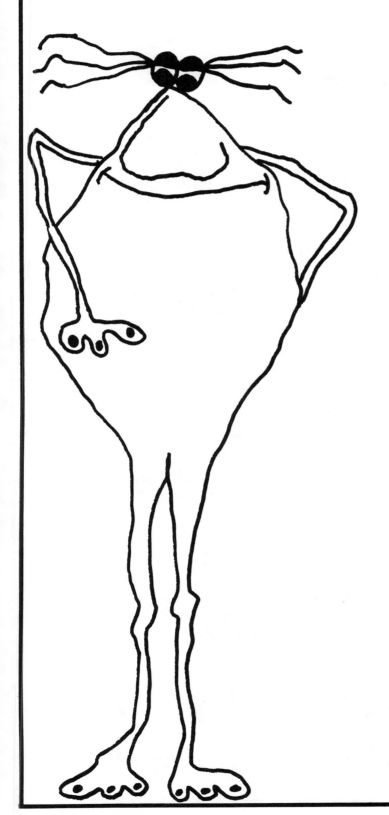

DIRECTIONS: The first player rolls the dice. He or she names the product of the two numbers shown on the dice. For example: If a player rolls a 5 and a 6, he crosses out the 30 on the score card. If a player has already crossed out the product of the numbers shown on the dice, he passes the dice to the next player and doesn't get to cross out any number. The game continues until one player has crossed out all 18 numbers on the score sheet.

To avoid competition, continue playing until each player has crossed out all the numbers on his or her score card.

CROSS OUT

1	2	3
4	5	6
8	9	10
12	15	16
18	20	24
25	30	36

SQUARE DEAL

Object: To control as much space on the grid as possible.

Materials: One pair of dice, two marking pens that are different colors and a single copy of the score card.

Directions: The first player rolls the dice. That player must then decide how to use the two numbers rolled. For example: If a player rolls a 2 and a 4, he has the option of marking the point either 2,4 or 4,2. When a player has successfully marked all four points of a square, he then draws a line connecting each of the four dots and fills in that area with the appropriate color. The game continues until all areas have been colored in or at least as much as possible. Some areas will not be claimed by either player because both players will have marked the corners with different colors.

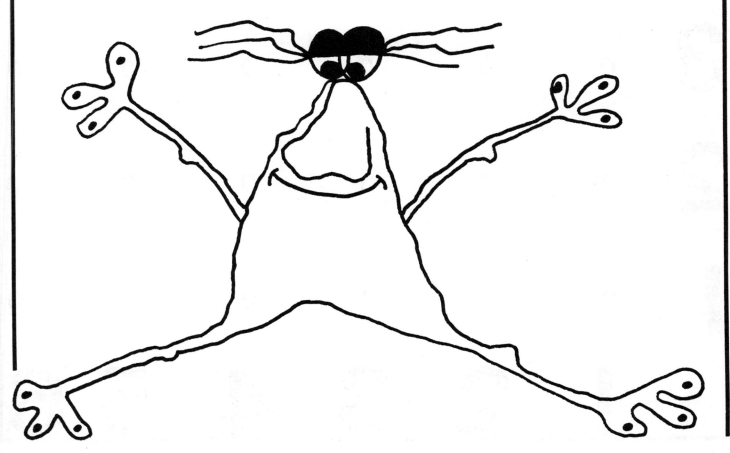

53

SQUARE DEAL
SCORE SHEET

	1	2	3	4	5	6
6	o	o	o	o	o	o
5	o	o	o	o	o	o
4	o	o	o	o	o	o
3	o	o	o	o	o	o
2	o	o	o	o	o	o
1	o	o	o	o	o	o

E.S.P.

Object: To test the ability of a friend's ESP (extrasensory perception) by using cards and keeping score.

Materials: Five ESP cards, two score sheets and two people

Directions: Decide which person will be the sender of the messages and which person will be the receiver. The players should sit facing one another. The sender and the receiver should have some way of covering the score sheets from each other. To begin the sender shuffles the five cards and turns one card face up. He then concentrates on this card and tries to send the mental picture to the receiver. Both persons then mark the score sheet with the appropriate shape. This procedure is repeated 24 more times. Check the score sheets to see how they compare. How many times did your friend get your message correct? Change places and the receiver becomes the sender and the sender becomes the receiver.

1.	plus	line	circle	square	star
2.	plus	line	circle	square	star
3.	plus	line	circle	square	star
4.	plus	line	circle	square	star
5.	plus	line	circle	square	star
6.	plus	line	circle	square	star
7.	plus	line	circle	square	star
8.	plus	line	circle	square	star
9.	plus	line	circle	square	star
10.	plus	line	circle	square	star
11.	plus	line	circle	square	star
12.	plus	line	circle	square	star
13.	plus	line	circle	square	star
14.	plus	line	circle	square	star
15.	plus	line	circle	square	star
16.	plus	line	circle	square	star
17.	plus	line	circle	square	star
18.	plus	line	circle	square	star
19.	plus	line	circle	square	star
20.	plus	line	circle	square	star
21.	plus	line	circle	square	star
22.	plus	line	circle	square	star
23.	plus	line	circle	square	star
24.	plus	line	circle	square	star
25.	plus	line	circle	square	star

ANSWER KEY

5 = 54	19 = 61
7 = 55	8 = 57
10 = 58	57 = 80
2 = 54	100 = 103
3 = 53	35 = 69
11 = 57	70 = 88
50 = 78	0 = 53
33 = 68	44 = 75

Page 2

Answers may vary:

$(7 \times 3) + 4 \div 5 + 6 - 10 = 1$

$10 + 9 + 1 \div 5 - 3 = 1$

$8 \times 6 \div 4 + 2 \div 7 - 1 = 1$

Page 3

$20 = 4 + 16$

$70 = 64 + 4 + (2 \times 1)$

$33 = (2 \times 16) + 1$

$40 = (2 \times 16) + (2 \times 4)$

$99 = 64 + (2 \times 16) + (3 \times 1)$

$130 = (64 \times 2) + (1 \times 2)$

$88 = 64 + 16 + (2 \times 4)$

$18 = 16 + (2 \times 1)$

$36 = (16 \times 2) + 4$

$207 = (64 \times 3) + (3 \times 4) + (3 \times 1)$

$400 = (6 \times 64) + 16$

$876 = (13 \times 64) + (2 \times 16) + (3 \times 4)$

$67 = 64 + (3 \times 1)$

$193 = (3 \times 64) + 1$

Page 4

$16 + 4 + 1 = 21$

$64 + (2 \times 1) = 66$

$64 + 16 + (3 \times 4) = 92$

$(4 \times 3) + 1 = 13$

$(64 \times 2) + (16 \times 3) + (4 \times 3) = 188$

$(64 \times 2) + (16 \times 2) + (4 \times 2) + (3 \times 1) = 171$

$(64 \times 3) + (4 \times 3) + 1 = 205$

$(4 \times 3) + (1 \times 3) = 15$

$(64 \times 3) + (16 \times 3) + (4 \times 2) + 1 = 249$

$(64 \times 3) + (16 \times 2) = 224$

$(64 \times 4) + (16 \times 3) + 4 + (1 \times 3) = 311$

Page 5

$11 + 11 - 1 - 1 - 1 = 19$

$22 \div 2 + 2 + 2 + 2 + 2 = 19$

$33 - 3 \div 3 + 3 + 3 + 3 = 19$

$44 \div 4 + 4 + 4 = 19$

$5 \times 5 - 5 \div 5 + 5 + 5 = 19$

$66 + 6 + 6 \div 6 + 6 = 19$

$7 \times 7 + 77 + 7 \div 7 = 19$

$88 \div 8 + 8 = 19$

$99 - 9 \div 9 + 9 = 19$

*Children should be shown the correct way to write equations. The answer shows the steps in order to get the answer and is not really an equation. For example: $\frac{22}{2} + 2 + 2 + 2 + 2 = 19$

Page 6

A	=	1
B	=	7
C	=	4
D	=	6
E	=	8
F	=	9
G	=	3
H	=	2
I	=	5

Page 7

$48 = 15, 16, 17$

$123 = 40, 41, 42$

$225 = 74, 75, 76$

$306 = 101, 102, 103$

$288 = 95, 96, 97$

$1,000 = 198, 199, 200, 201, 202$

$500 = 98, 99, 100, 101, 102$

$700 = 138, 139, 140, 141, 142$

$400 = 78, 79, 80, 81, 82$

$300 = 58, 59, 60, 61, 62$

$995 = 197, 198, 199, 200, 201$

$15 = 1, 2, 3, 4, 5$

Page 8

1. 16
2. 512
3. 1:15
4. 1,048,576
5. 3:00
6. 2,097,152
7. 16,777,216
8. 67,108,864
9. 2:45
10. 268,435,456

Page 9

1.
$$\begin{array}{r} 888 \\ 88 \\ 8 \\ 8 \\ +\ 8 \\ \hline 1,000 \end{array}$$

2. $4 + 4\ 4/4 = 9$

3. $1 + 2 + 3 = 6$
$1 \times 2 \times 3 = 6$

4. $14\ \frac{14}{14}$ or $16 - \frac{16}{16}$

5. Answer will vary $6 + \frac{6}{6}$

6. $1 + 2 + 34 + 56 + 7 = 100$

Page 10

$4 \times 4 =$ 9 7 2 4 (1 6) 7 8 9
$5 \times 5 =$ 9 3 (2 0 + 5) 6 3 4
$6 \times 19 =$ 8 0 4 1 4 (1 1 4) 3 3 7
$7 \times 75 =$ 7 (5 0 0 + 2 0 + 5) 7 8 8
$1000 - 1 =$ 7 8 9 1 1 6 (1 1 1 × 9) 7
$15 \times 15 =$ 2 0 0 (4 5 × 5) 6 2 2 0 9
$492 \div 6 =$ 9 8 0 (4 1 × 2) 5 6 7 7
$441 + 141 =$ 5 8 (3 9 0 + 1 9 2) 6 7 8
$1143 + 1945 =$ (1 6 × 1 9 3) 7 3 0 0 6 8
$88 \times 37 =$ (6 1 6 + 2 6 4 0) 5 9 6 7
$1000 + 50 =$ 7 8 (7 5 × 1 4) 6 8 9 1 3 5
$196 \div 14 =$ (7 × 2) 4 6 8 7 1 7 4 5 9 8 0

Page 11

The numbers in each row can be in any order

Ted: 206, 45, 45, 39, 39, 19, 19,
Jeff: 192, 45, 45, 45, 19, 19, 19
Mitch: 180, 45, 39, 39, 19, 19, 19
Ann: 242, 50, 50, 45, 39, 39, 19
Eddie: 252, 45, 45, 45, 39, 39, 39

Page 12

2,521

Page 13

0 = x
1 = h
2 = n
3 = g
4 = w
5 = j
6 = q
7 = z
8 = f
9 = v

Page 14

hats $2.00
dresses $5.00
shoes $4.00

Page 15

1. $15.00
2. $20.00
3. 300
4. 100
5. 50¢
6. ¼

Page 16

horses, 10
cows, 20
chickens, 20

Page 17

1. $5, $1, $1, $1, $1 = $9 in 5 rolls
2. $5, 25¢, 25¢, 25¢, 25¢ = $6 in 5 rolls
3. 25¢, 25¢, 25¢, 25¢, 25¢, 25¢, 25¢, 25¢ = $2 in 8 rolls
4. $5, $5, $1 = $11 in 3 rolls

(There will not be an answer for every roll combination)

Page 18

1. 3 minutes
2. twice, at 12:30 p.m., 1:00 p.m., 1:30 p.m., & 12:30 a.m., 1:00 a.m., 1:30 a.m.

Page 19

1. 2
2. 4
3. 1
4. between 10:45 & 11:00
5. from
6. to
7. Mary
8. Jim
9. Mary
10. Jim

Page 20

1. 1,200 eggs
2. 50 eggs
3. 4 weeks
4. 4 weeks
5. 10 weeks

Page 21

1. 36
2. 6
3. 84
4. 24
5. 20
6. 30
7. 30
8. 6
9. 47
10. 31

Page 22

Andrew is 25
Ruth is 25
Kathy is 5
Tim is 5
Rose is 5
(the children are triplets)

Page 23

a = 1/8
b = 1/16
c = 1/8
d = 3/16
e = 1/16
f = 1/16
g = 1/32
h = 1/32
i = 1/64

Page 24

1. 200
2. 100
3. 50
4. 250

Page 25

Betty has 12 beans.
George has 28 beans.
Mary has 2 beans.
Peter has 14 beans.

Page 26

There are 2 dogs.
There is 1 cat.
There are 12 horses.
There are 6 chickens.

Page 27

1 1/12 is chocolate.
1 11/12 is white.
$4/12 + 3/12 + 6/12 = \frac{13}{12} = 1\ 1/12$

Page 28

	24 oz.	13 oz.	11 oz.	5 oz.
begin	24	0	0	0
	0	8	11	5
	16	8	0	0
	16	0	08	0
	3	13	8	0
	3	8	8	5
	8	8	8	0

Page 29

All records have one long groove.

Page 30

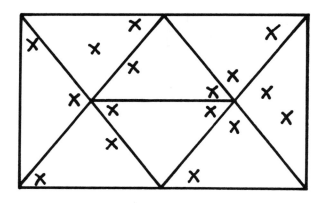

Page 31

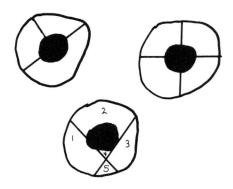

Page 32

1.   7
        3
     9,1,5,8,2
        6
        4

2.   9,1,5
     8,4,3
     7,6,2

Page 33

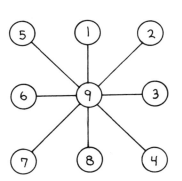

Page 34

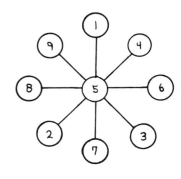

58

Page 35

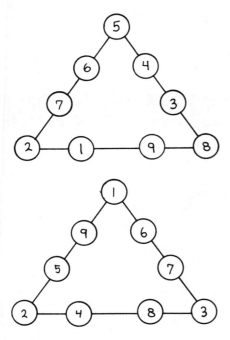

Page 36

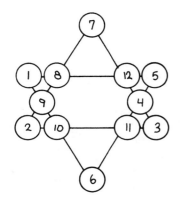

Page 37

Just so the ten is in the middle and the connecting outside circles total 30.

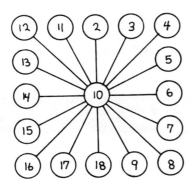

Page 38

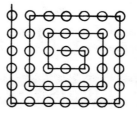

Page 39

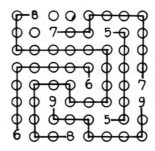

Page 40

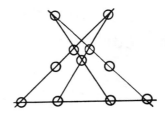

Page 41

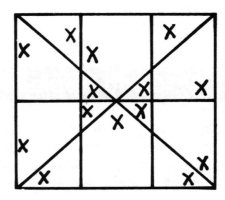

Page 43

B
F
H
G,E,D,F,I,C

59

The Growing Family of Good Apple Products and Services Includes

4 Periodicals to Meet the Needs of Educators

BIG, Beautiful Activities That Work as Hard as You Do

The Good Apple Newspaper, for grades 2-8, offers practical ready-to-use reproducibles, seasonal activities, posters, games and ideas. Our working teacher /authors know how to motivate and reinforce basic skills. Let us brighten your classroom and challenge young minds. Bigger, more colorful, and free of outside advertising, *The Good Apple Newspaper* is your best value in teaching publications.

Timesaving Ideas Ready to "Challenge" the Gifted!

Challenge provides you with ready-to-use creative and critical thinking activities, articles from leaders in gifted education and features to help parents of gifted students. Inspiring interviews, thought-provoking games and complete units of study provide you with in-depth materials to "challenge" the academic, physical, mechanical and artistically gifted child.

Teachers Love Lollipops!

Lollipops magazine is especially for teachers of preschool-grade 2. Each issue includes stories and poems, calendars, bulletin boards, value-related materials, a full-color poster and more. The seasonal focus of each issue provides you with learning material children will love.

Finally! A Ready-to-Use Teaching Magazine

Oasis magazine, from Good Apple, is packed full of timesaving, skill-building activities and ideas just for you—the busy teacher of grades 5-9. Reproducibles, activities, teacher tips, full-color posters, calendars and reviews are all age and curriculum appropriate! With more you'll really use and no outside advertising, there's no better value in a classroom magazine.

Good Apple Idea and Activity Books

In all subject areas for all grade levels, preschool-grade 8+. Idea books, activity books, bulletin board books, units of instruction, reading, creativity, readiness, gameboards, science, math, social studies, responsibility education, self-concept, gifted, seasonal ideas, arts/crafts, poetry, language arts and teacher helpers.

Activity Posters • Note Pads • Software • Videos

Teachers Publishing for Teachers